Library of
Davidson College

THE HOURS OF MORNING

POEMS 1976-1979

THE HOURS OF MORNING

William Carpenter

POEMS 1976-79

University Press of Virginia   Charlottesville

THE UNIVERSITY PRESS OF VIRGINIA
Copyright © 1981 by the Rector and Visitors
of the University of Virginia

First published 1981

Library of Congress Cataloging in Publication Data

Carpenter, William.
  The hours of morning.

  (The Virginia Commonwealth University series for
contemporary poetry ; 1980)
  I. Title. II. Series: Virginia Commonwealth University
series for contemporary poetry ; 1980.
PS3553.A7622H6   811'.54   81-7452
ISBN 0-8139-0909-0   AACR2

Printed in the United States of America

For James and Dorothy Carpenter
my parents

FOREWORD

"It is time to cast off sophistication," William Carpenter says, early on in this sane and searching book.

> The prettiness
> of things is like bird feathers. The butcher knows,
> plucking as he does on weekdays while the kids
>
> walk by. He handles the bare bird,
> the bones. He gives the cows' sad eyes
> to his own cat, pure Abyssinian.

The appeal of these poems lies for me in their particularity, their willingness to handle the bare bird, their evident caring about the universe, the animal kingdom, human kinship, and, with becoming diffidence, love. What it comes down to, finally, is a matter of congeniality. Carpenter's voice speaks to my sensibilities. The world as he sees it perplexes him much as it perplexes me. When I read him, I feel buttressed by our shared feelings.

Many of these poems explore the individual's sense of isolation from society. Sometimes the poet speaks; sometimes a persona is doing the thinking and feeling. In "Taken from Van Gogh" the painter's severed ear comes to stand for the struggle to communicate: "Trying to reach the heart, trying to give / we slice off pieces of ourselves like fruit." In "The Equinox and After" the persona resists the loosening effects of spring on his solitary life: "Winter was a long novel read by kerosene / beside the stove." April, however,

> is the birthday party
> of the world and you are the downstairs tenant,
> beating your broom against the ceiling.

Or this excerpt from the long title poem, a meditation about the poet's life and love:

> The city is a hospital without patients.
> Millions of doctors in the streets,
> thousands of doctors taking the subway,
> hundreds of doctors in airplanes
> over the city, piloted by doctors.
> It is no wonder that we are diseased,
> living like this on a remote island,
> living on an island with blue herons
> standing beside the road like guards.
> The island is a hospital without doctors.

My favorites in this collection are Carpenter's "Five Translations from the Poems of Anasim Miscjek," translations, he tells us, without originals, "Miscjek being perhaps the idea of a Rumanian poet with whom I feel affinities." Such a disclaimer allows the poet a broad acre to roam, from the small disquiet of an angel imprisoned in the bourgeois apartment of a commissar to an epistolatory diatribe directed against the defector-brother in America. Perhaps most chilling, the poem titled "Miscjek's Success" contains a vision beyond the poet's "remote border province," where he lives on a state pension, of barbarians who emerge from the forest:

> I see they have hollowed the heads
> of animals to wear on their own heads. . . .
> Unholy languages drift on the night wind,
> one of which is my own. My ears stand up,
> I smell something like the smell of blood.
> I feel my throat forming the alien sounds.

Carpenter, like Cavafy, declaiming without shrillness, reminds us that despite our social standing we are never far from "the alien sounds." Indeed, in a poem that seems a summation of all else in this book, the poet reminds us

> It seems we have lived before,
> as immigrants in the dark hold of a ship, . . .
> that we exchange

> bodies for a moment and then labor on
> like birds stemming the wind. There is no end
> to the design. Death is a blue figure
> somewhere in the tapestry.

These are poems that confirm us in our human frailty, our questing appetites, our need always to search out the germ of order in the chaos of emotion. They stand up well to scrutiny.

Maxine Kumin

ACKNOWLEDGMENTS

The author and publisher wish to thank the following magazines, where certain poems first appeared:

The Beloit Poetry Journal, 29, no. 4 (Summer 1979), for "The Yacht," reprinted by permission of the editor; reprinted as the Pablo Neruda Prize Poem in *Nimrod,* 23, no. 1 (Fall/Winter 1979).

Hiram Poetry Review, no. 23 (Winter 1977), for "The Man Who Built a Car," reprinted by permission of the editors; reprinted as the Henry Dumas Prize Poem in no. 24 (Spring 1978).

New England Review, 2, no. 2 (Fall 1979), for "A Portrait of Edward Hopper."

New Maine Writing II, 1979, Maine–New England Small Press Association, for "A Little Nightmusic," reprinted by permission.

Quarry West 1 (1980), for "California."

CONTENTS

Foreword by Maxine Kumin	vii
Acknowledgments	x
The Early Snow	1
The Yacht	3
Snake Music	8
Stopping at Tulsa	10
War and Peace	12
Cézanne at Mont Sainte-Victoire	13
The Man Who Built a Car	16
Friends of de Chirico	18
A Little Nightmusic	19
Autumn Encounter	22
A Portrait of Edward Hopper	24
The Artist's Hand	24
Evening Wind	24
Nighthawks	25
Gas	26
"Autumn" from *Living in the North*	27
Giacometti	29
The Keeper	30
The Man with Pipe: Twelve Songs	32
Still Lives	36
Picking Up a Spoon	38
Taken from Van Gogh	41
The Equinox and After	44
Dentist	46
Five Translations from the Poems of Anasim Miscjek	47
The Commissars	47
Angel	48
To His Brother in America	49
Prison Song	50
Miscjek's Success	51

California	52
A Station of Monet	54
Running in Winter	56
Romance	59
The *Grand Design*	62
Poem on His Birthday	65
The Hours of Morning	66

THE HOURS OF MORNING

POEMS 1976-1979

The dream has the structure of a sentence.
—JACQUES LACAN

The Early Snow

It begins falling after
midnight. We are still up,
arguing over seeds, over
the failure of this year's garden
and all the failures.
The snow falls on my stunted
cornstalks, on your strange
Mexican-looking lupine.
It bends the delphinium
like a white giraffe
with its neck broken
but its body still upright.
The articles of summer,
tractor and bicycle, begin
to change. The snow restores
them to their origins
when they were pure metal
and white hot from the forge.
We walk in the snow ourselves,
the air unnaturally warm,
the flakes wet and heavy
feeling like drowned birds
in our hands.
We take off our shirts
and stand there face to face.
The snow bleaches your hair

like an old woman's.
The space between your breasts
fills up with snow and runs over.
It gathers your feet into the earth
like the roots of a white birch.
When I finally go in to sleep,
soaked through and shivering,
it is alone.

The Yacht

1 It is a space in the sea's eye, it is
one gesture among points of light: that sail
this morning, white laceration of cold blue.

When I think of freedom I think of Li Ch'eng;
I think of the spirit of things, and the spirit's
resonance in itself. I think of an old man

painting, and the hand painting an old man
by his tree. I think till I am old myself

and a woman's shadow pushes a slim brush
across my skin, a mask for the new season
where we become the events of dawn and night

as a green snake glides into the spring grass,
becomes the grass: one word, this Tuesday,
moving among words on a clear page.

2 There is so little at the center of things.
I look through you and there is the air
whispering from another place. The earth

around you I have seen in its twelve seasons,
whose form is the first mirror, the mirage
of vision, a civilized man appalled

by the clown costume wearing his own face.
Unbearable center, only in spring do you
reveal these fingers, spectacles of light.

3   Astonished to be here again, I take off
    my eyes, I walk the alleys of this world
    as a deaf mute, smelling and tasting.

    Why do I think obsessively of bodies
    and of the possibilities of night
    as I pass through a simple forest hearing

    these warblers and looking them up in my book?
    Free doctor, psychoanalyst of birds,
    I scan their bright derangements for a clue.

    To live here is not to be wholly sane.
    Poor Septimus was right, everything is alive
    and God is love. I am liable to arrest

    by the particularities of order,
    dangerous to creation, fat man
    absurd and ponderous, specialist in time

    alone and death, sex specialist, someone intrigued
    with bones, promiscuous invalid, living
    for one season only, the man of spring.

4   It is time to cast off sophistication
    and prepare the final self, as a French painter
    might sell his pet iguana and become

    Christian on the eve of his wife's death.
    I am a single person cutting grass,
    one who is still surprised by a young snake

    under the machine, the tail severed neatly,
    the rest whistling into the field. The prettiness
    of things is like bird feathers. The butcher knows,
    plucking as he does on weekdays while the kids

walk by. He handles the bare bird,
the bones. He gives the cows' sad eyes
to his own cat, pure Abyssinian.

Scattered upon his block is the truth of it,
the significance of flesh, we used to say,
poultry without facade, gifts of the heart.

5   Over and over. A woman butchers a pig.
Bird hearts, a dozen sparrows roasted
for a dime; the East Side of New York

when Audubon lived there, a cowpath, half
a hundred farms, an eagle resting on the wind.

It is in all living things; the speed alone
distinguishes their dying, the short-billed wren
and the old tamaracks, drifting that way together.

6   I am at breakfast with three patriarchs
this morning: Li Ch'eng, the butcher,
and my great-uncle who ran the funeral home.

The talk comes round to sausage, a motif
I struggled to avoid without success,

which is perhaps the real thing truly murdered,
a figure of decline since the Sung dynasty,
the finished product, stupid, in an age of chance.

7   (*The butcher himself sings this*)

Now and tomorrow, bone and flesh, song
in the heart, the knife falling
among bones, the bones falling

miraculously apart, something inside
humming like metal. Beyond ornithology
I have known birds, I have known

animals. One or two faces I do
remember, the rest whistle by
like geese traveling the spring air.

8 Faces are travelers. The body stays at home
like a pair of fat trees in the underbrush,
unplanned and not too beautiful.

Circling like ospreys above the fact,
we might find it again and we might not.
It would depend upon the weather, it would

depend upon ourselves, it would depend
upon the status of our preparations.
I have seen it happen for two people

walking a woods path among tamaracks,
the first strawberries quilting the damp ground.
To reach a center, to find it is not air,

to know that we are there and breathing there
something beyond air, to relinquish all control,
to wait, to strike at the apt time, to find

words for that silence; that is a day's labor
and a night. It is all a meatcutter could do,
laying his knife aside, to reconstruct

his animals, remake their faces, to place
the brain just so, the tongues in their quiet throats,
to light the eyes again and give them breath,

to send them out by rows into the night,
the new herd finally uttering from his shop
to low softly and forage the streets for grass.

Snake Music

1   The boy brings a dozen pet snakes
aboard the airplane in a shopping bag,
then falls asleep. At thirty thousand feet,
a snake comes out, sneaks past the seat ahead,
and then another. It is a night flight
and the plane is dark. The passengers
feel the cool snakes slide past their legs;
they wake with horror to the whole plane
crawling with snakes, their two worst fears
fulfilled at once: reptiles and flight.
A hundred human bodies contract as one
in the dark shock of recognition.
The plane shudders in the stratosphere.
The hostesses call the pilot, who comes
back to round them up. The craft
flies on undamaged, but the boy
wakes at sunrise to an empty bag.
He cries silently for his lost snakes;
the plane begins descending.

2   In Oklahoma there are rattlesnakes
on every lawn, in every patch of brush
on the bare plain, in people's garages,
behind the lawnmower, under the laundry sink.
In August, when the land is hot
their men go forth to round them up in bags
and place them in the city swimming pool,
which they have drained for the occasion.
On that warm evening the boys come out
bearing their pistols for the Rattlesnake Shoot.
They fire into the pool of living snakes
till nothing moves, then scoop the bodies out
and fry them up in special copper pans.
The long Oklahoma night is shattered
by the sound of men consuming snakes and beer.
That is the Rattlesnake Fry.
The snakes enter the bodies of the men
and after midnight they grow quieter.
There are no snakes in that wide countryside
but men, wearing the faces of reptiles,
begin to dance, slowly at first, embracing
each other in their beefy arms,
licking with slick and quick forked tongues
the face beside them.
After the Shoot and Fry
they hold the Rattlesnake Dance.
Each man has come full circle, crouched
on the dry sand, arms at his sides,
his tail in his cool green mouth.

Stopping at Tulsa

For Manly and Mary Johnson

1   These western cities
concentrate the land
like powerful mushrooms.
They gather it to themselves
through black rhizomes, feeding
the place of government.
As the jet banks and descends
into the Tulsa airport,
I think of another city,
Siena, the utopian frescoes
in the *Palazzo Pubblico*
by Ambrogio Lorenzetti,
those peasants driving their animals
into the walled city,
the nobles riding into the fields
to hunt. One of them holds
a falcon on his gloved wrist.
His wife, riding beside him, has
the face of a Sienese Madonna.
His dogs are on the scent,
tails high, noses to the ground.
Behind them, against the sky,
workmen finish the cathedral,
a tonsured monk serves mass
to a small group. In Siena
it was all numinous:
the men spading the olive grove,
the mules packing expensive goods
through the close streets,
the woman with her tambourine
and the dark swineherd.

2   In Tulsa I noticed something
    unusual. The man taking my bags
    was in disguise. The women
    at the car rental booth
    were wearing wigs. Under
    their street clothes were
    their other clothes,
    inside their bodies
    they wore armatures.
    On the way from the Tulsa airport
    I passed a Tower of Prayer
    next to a pair of praying hands
    five stories high.
    In the streets, the old Indians
    moved through the crowd,
    their bodies painted for war,
    their feathered headdresses
    reaching the sidewalk.
    Where I stayed in Tulsa
    the house began to change
    at midnight. I lay awake.
    I heard resonances
    as if the living room
    opened directly into the earth.
    There was the sound of the floor
    moving and moving back,
    there were guests arriving
    that did not leave.
    Tulsa is just past the edge
    of Central Time;
    the morning was very dark.
    I looked at my own face
    being shaved, my own hand
    holding the razor.
    They were like nothing
    I had ever seen.

War and Peace

The man approaching us is Pierre Bezhukov.
He keeps coming closer, in that Russian way
that makes us smell cheap vodka on his breath
and certain other smells, deeper and muskier.
He has been at Anatole's again. There have been
women. There has been dancing with a bear.
We can see bear's fur on his huge shoulders.
Who could take such a man seriously?
There has to be great suffering, he says.
There has to be a home, more than a home,
a land, a place repeating in itself
our history, our first ill-chosen wife,
our duel at sunrise, the long, primitive war
with its strange ending and Andrew Bolkonski dead.

Cézanne at Mont Sainte-Victoire

He faced a mountain without
trees, in dead winter.
To the French mind
it was a geometry of ice,
a mountain that came apart
like a wooden horse,
an army of cubes inside
that could destroy the world.

I go up to Katahdin
in late October,
a dark season,
the trees bare already,
my family caving in,
a light first snow
covering the land.

A pileated woodpecker
crosses between trees;
I stop my car in admiration.
Its red crest
is an opening of fire.

The night before,
a young physicist
lectured on singularities.
Now there is no space, only
the unceasing storm of events.
I walk round and round
in the motel
thinking of Planck's constant.

I see the event horizon
through which we fall
into the speed of light
and reverse ourselves in time,
infinitely extended
and traveling towards a birth.

I think I am there already,
the times that I speak to you
and you hear nothing,
only the sound of light
whispering past.
It comes back to one person
standing before a mountain.
It is Marsden Hartley
before Katahdin,
sad lover of men,
who died in Gouldsboro,
Maine, fifty miles eastward
but still in our own landscape.
It is Ansel Adams
on snowshoes in Yosemite
his face under the cloth,
the Half Dome inverted
in the ground glass.
It is Cézanne
at Mont Sainte-Victoire,
it is the unmoved
crystalline surface
of the rock,
it is the opened rock
turning inside.
It is this granite ledge,
these silent Canada Jays
scratching for food.

Unbirdlike, they walk
over the bare stone,
they know nothing
of Mount Katahdin,
they show no fear
of the unknown:
the cold shadows
of mountains,
this other species.

The Man Who Built a Car

At the Flea Market in Eastport, Maine,
the same vendors return week after week
with brass lanterns and green-crusted cuspidors,
elaborate andirons with the faces of bishops,
axe handles, antique spades, ships' wheels,
candelabra, Victorian love seats,
parrot cages and the wardrobes of women
who died in the thirties and forties.
There is also the man with the car,
building his own car over the years
from the broken facts of his world.
At last he has offered it to the public eye.
It has International Harvester wheels.
It has the body of an elegant teak speedboat,
an airplane propeller and a strange cabin
of two telephone booths bolted together.
It will go, he claims, anywhere. It is the
true amphibian, though he tows it to Eastport
with a regular truck. The car changes subtly:
a television antenna, a stuffed golden eagle,
a window box, then a row of geraniums
looking as if a woman had moved in.
It grows clearer and clearer.
It will not go anywhere. It is his home.
He secretly lives in it, though living
at the Flea Market is not allowed.

It is not even for sale. That
was a deception. It is his life;
it contains a bronzed teething ring
and a typewriter. In the cabin, below decks,
his wife is tiled into the mosaic wall,
his children are seated around the table
forever, like a group death from Pompeii.
Now he is building a door out of oak planks.
He intends to seal himself in like a Pharoah.
He has elaborate plans for his own death.
If the car is unsold, he will drive it into the sun.
It will begin to move slowly, the propeller
beating the air, tires ribbing the earth,
boat's prow pointed skyward, the family inside
strapped down like astronauts for the long journey.

Friends of de Chirico

In this painting, *Mysteries of the Street*,
a young girl in sunlight balances
her hoop in the clean Italian square.
Arched doorways, a long arcade
like the *ospedale* near San Marco.
Even the shadows seem correct,
one shadow for each object, falling
on the side opposite the sun.
Everything is correct except one thing:
there is no meaning.

It is how things become when we are dead.
The shadows appear more real than the event:
The day your husband left, his shoes
and clothes gone from the cedar chest,
no forwarding address, your life abandoned.
You turned to the high window and the child
was there, pushing her hoop through shadows
of high buildings, and that was death.
You coiled into the patterns of your life,
dusted the clock, locked the tall casement,
moved like a spider in its barren web.

A Little Nightmusic

It is one night and every night
I sleep with you
I am the faceless man in your dream
you are in my dream as the bird shadow
walking beside me
I sleep with you
because it is October
because the earth is a night traveler
and the calendar is coming upon us
I sleep with you
we are particles in intergalactic space
we are remnants of the primal explosion
we experience the big bang
in our own way
I sleep with you
the ancestors watch over us
though they are long dead their eyes
have learned to see through the dark
I sleep with you
since death is in the corner of the room
dressed as a tortoise-shell cat
since we are still animals
only this time with voices
since your back startles me always
like a snake skeleton
hidden in sand
I sleep with you
you call us snails without shells

I sleep with you
we have slept with others
who are with us now and forever
I sleep with you
it is the breaking of a stern commandment
we must also bring this one from the mountain
we must carve it in stone
and place it beside the other
we must look on them both with a cold eye
I sleep with you
to honor my mother and father
and your mother and your father
who is in heaven
I sleep with you
we are the roots of trees tangled in the earth
our hands are nocturnal lizards
gone blind over the centuries
I sleep with you
we have spoken in hatred
the sword has come down between us
our words were ice picks
in the delicate heart tissue
I sleep with you
as Plato and Alcibiades
in the warm Athenian night
as King Lear and his lost wife
as comrades on the eve of the revolution
as the enemy over the trenches
readies for the dawn attack
I sleep with you
in the clothes of my own skin
I wear with you only
your clothes are my arms and legs
the color of dried leaves

I sleep with you
as two marionettes
fine wires connect us
to the eccentric stars
I sleep with you
in a night broken by strange energies
the imperfections of my body
and the imperfections of your body
like two continents drifting together
I sleep with you
in the principle of uncertainty
I look for you
you change into myself
I sleep alone
the red star rises again
in Scorpio
one constellation

Autumn Encounter

The deer stop in my headlights, knowing it is either dawn or death. The three of them wander in the road as if it were a night meadow. They wear the features of women hypnotized with light. I dim the switch. They weave themselves into the trees and return as others, darker and tamer than before. I could reach out the open window and touch their faces; I could take their lives one after another, they are so close. They have come forth for contact and I fail, having the wrong language. They wait a while confused, then walk from the moonlit edges to the dense forest. I raise my hand against their going, as I had raised it the day you turned for the last time and left my room.

Behind the houses of the poor, the deer hang by their hind legs. The tongues are cut out and laid on stones behind the carcasses. Their throats are slit and the blood on the snow freezes, the way children would make an iced drink by pouring raspberry syrup on the snow. The eyes of the dead deer forgive us nothing. They are like the eyes of women; they carry the whole history of our relation.

On the Maine Turnpike in November the deer are stretched over the bodies of cars, or frozen solid and fastened to the rack like skis. I have seen cars with the trunk full of deer and the heads pulled out so their ears could be pierced by the game inspectors. The men in the cars are drunk; they drink in order to forget a sexual act in the dark forest. They have been intimate with animals, and afterwards have taken their lives with hollowpoint bullets and telescopic sights.

What were the deer asking? Had they come to me for killing, to offer the delicate muscles of their throats to the knife I did not have? Though they came in expectation, I did not kill. They return silently to the trees. The air thickens with disappointment as I engage the gears and drive forward to my house.

In the Cave of the Three Brothers the first artist sketches a man with a deer's head and upright penis: the Animal Master, who crosses that alien bridge and returns dancing, who bears the stag's energy to his own people. He is the schizophrenic of the tribe, the outcast. The man painting him is another cripple, who draws by torchlight while the hunters burn meadows to drive the game into the ravine. Ten thousand years ago we knew the secret of the deer. We put on its bleeding head and danced by starlight, naked and aroused. We dressed our bodies with thick animal tails. I study this image in the safety of a book, washed with electric light. I run my finger over the glossy plate and shiver with recognition.

A Portrait of Edward Hopper

1 *The Artist's Hand (Three Views)*

He sits before the mirror and draws his hand
three times. It is a slim ascetic hand
begging to God. It is a confidence man
putting his hand out for the take;
it is a blind squid with a wrist watch
climbing from a black hole. Watch out
for a hand in the mirror. It is not your own,
it has tendencies, secretly it hates
the painting hand, as you hate the woman
behind you in the mirror, the dark,
the sinister one, the left side of your life,
the place you came from, the Siamese twin:
three shocking views of your own paw.

2 *Evening Wind*

The young model undressed before the poet
who stood with pen and notebook and made words
like lines, phrases like shadows in a woodcut.
He knelt her on the bed in the dollar hotel.
The damp city wind blew back the curtains;
she started up, her hair fell on her breasts,
her hand touched the mattress like a cat's foot.
He worked on metaphors. The evening window
was a white paper, smells entered like words
from the young city, the smell of the steam
railroad, the smell of the delicatessen
on Tenth Street, the smell of animals

carried through the streets. What did she hear
on the bleak wind? The room was full of senses.
There was a strange man behind her shadow.
It was the poet with his book of fear,
writing and writing in her intimate space.
She saw and covered herself.
She folded her head into her arms and wept.

3   *Nighthawks*

The Professor of Art History points
to the black space behind the figures
with his beam of light. It fills with men
in suits, with women laughing and dogs
trotting behind them. He turns it off;
they vanish. We are left with the truth:
a young man with a cigarette, his girl
eating a Fig Newton, an older man,
with glasses, facing them. The boy working
behind the counter bends like a white turtle
forever. His words are a five-cent cigar,
a cash register, a slant of moonlight,
a clean, frightening street. His friends are urns,
a male urn with coffee and a female urn with hot
water for tea. At sunrise he will pass through
the yellow door with the small window into another
picture; that awful darkness will be light again.

4 Gas

It might have been Rene Magritte. It was Hopper
on the furthest edge, every part of the painting
in a different time, blue sky, electric lights,
that terrible black road. What is the man
doing with his hands, is he putting the hose away,
after filling us, is it ourselves heading for Truro
in the Studebaker? October nineteen-forty,
the month that I was born, midway between
Poland and Pearl Harbor. I have examined this
all morning long for clues to my own birth,
as if I waited for a certain car
to enter on the left, for my own father
to ask that man for gas or for directions.
I drift too deeply into my own life,
being too much alone. Hopper, the artist,
chose Mobilgas because its Flying Horse
symbolized art, leapt out of history, bore
no man's saddle. Pegasus, there on the Cape, flew
into evening. Somewhere a woman was in labor:
only a few men knew what night would come.

"Autumn" from *Living in the North*

for Steve Katona

This morning they are putting away the whales.
As always, it is a vast operation.
The long line of whales almost reaches the horizon.
The orderlies slide the whale-car on its old rails
into the sea, the men in boats coax the whales
into alignment with the car. They fasten on the ropes.
You can see how the whale has come to rest squarely
on the timbers. It is not made to be in the air;
without support the bones and sides would collapse.
It would die of its own weight.
They have done this year after year, in autumn,
and their fathers and grandfathers before them,
for there is no emigration from here, and they marry
mostly their own kind. I myself came from away,
but I see my own son in one of the small boats,
appeasing the whales, keeping them in the line
as they wait out the slow craft of being hauled,
as they abide their transit from the first waters
into the cold air. They are hauling the whales
and the whole town gathers before sunrise.
An abnormal tide laps at the road itself
as they open the doors to the whale-houses
and begin moving them in.
The breathing of dry whales is slow,
their vapor smells of the inside of the sea,
and the natives say on the day that they haul whales
you can feel heartbeats in the earth
even as you drive your car over the road.

Evening descends suddenly in the whale yard.
We are cleaning the last of them with wire brooms,
for the whale carries a whole civilization on its back,
mussels and crabs and grass. One of the boys
finds a small octopus and we jump back
as if he had shown us a death's head.
When the last whale is moved into its shed,
as far as we can see, the ocean is empty.
A small flight of geese crosses the surface;
nothing remains inside. We close the doors,
we begin banking foundations for the long winter.

Giacometti

She took off her dress
before the mirror.
There was a blue parrot
making human sounds,
making the first movements
of recognition,
a parrot dancing at the thought
of its own image,
its actual self,
her self, imitating
a naked woman,
her eyes blank as the planets
her body flapping its long wings
in a corner of the ceiling,
her clothes draped care-
lessly on the chair.

The Keeper

I forget everything. I forget faces,
I forget the plots of movies, how
anything turned out, who is divorced
what couples are having an affair.
I am not fit to be alone.
You say I am like the Baron de Charlus
who could never be outside without
his keeper. I should have a keeper,
one of those unsmiling plainclothed men
that form circles around the President.
He would be physically large, he would
be trained in Chinese methods of restraint
for times when I forgot myself at parties
or began speaking aloud in the public street.
He would have reproducible features; he could
stand in at the annual family picture.
He would remind me of my lectures. In time
he would begin giving the lectures himself
while I sat attentively in the first row.
He would grow rabbinical with learning,
the keeper, he would grow old,
bits of food would appear in his thick beard
like insects; there would be insects
in his beard. He would accept all
my insomnia, he would lie there in the night
recalling the details of my life,
baffled with guilt, baffled with failing
to reach out when things went by.

It would be good sleeping while he stared
into the night. It would be good dreaming
of a simple, phenomenal world,
of the great translucent forms of giraffes.
It would be good to rise, like an idiot,
in a morning totally new, it would be the body
of the keeper beside the door, it would be
his death on the last day and not my own.
It would be I who kept on living here
and kept forgetting.

The Man with Pipe: Twelve Songs

1   Life is a stone, she said.
He was involved in thought,
he did not care.
The moon rose early. Her words
circled the afternoon
like vultures. He was glad
to be inside.

2   She touched him in a place
that made him think.
What was it like when
we went dancing and when death
was fat, our own kind uncle
dressed in his baggy trousers
and amusing hat?

3   Across two chairs he lay
asleep. His pipe was out,
a book was on his knee.
Outside the window
the cat played with a bird;
within the garden was a stone
bordered with grass.
There he was free.

4   It was the first of spring.
He took his pipe and stick
out to the stone and sat.
The stone became a head
and spoke. It said
what he had wanted to have
said, but the event
shuffled his bones.
He crossed himself in case
someone was looking.

5   His friends! He gives them beer.
Ideas circle the room like bats.
His pipe smolders and smokes
and talks. He pisses in the yard
and boils the cold stone.
Finally they leave: laughter
and boots in the snow,
their engines start,
their taillights
focus the night.

6   It is the crow again
walking the chimney.
It is the crow calling
at sunrise, the sound
from the fireplace.
Voices of former tenants
obscure his dreams.
The pipe lies on its side
breathing the air.

7   He sat naked. He smoked.
    The house was bare, winter
    had killed the trees,
    it was back down
    to nothing: man and his beast,
    the cat, fire, the pipe,
    this house, the head
    dreaming of women,
    herds of them
    grazing in the sun.

8   At church he checks his pipe
    in at the door. He hums
    the hymn, he counts the heads,
    the sun comes through stained glass
    into his lap. Good.
    God must be good, and after,
    when we die, things
    will be easy, as the man had said.
    His right foot falls asleep.

9   It rains all night and rains
    the next day. He stokes his pipe
    inverted. He walks
    in a damp road.
    Next month
    a raincoat
    make love three times
    in the same night.
    Spring resolutions.

10   He dies. He comes to life.
     The pipe goes on and off,
     the stars revolve.
     The clock slows down,
     a meteor falls
     and cools into a stone.
     He brings trowel and spade,
     he plants crocuses
     in broken circles.

11   It all tastes vile.
     He sits and puffs
     and shuts his eyes
     like a stone man.
     He can't go up
     he can't go back.
     Sad man, sad pipe:
     life has gone south,
     only the crow remains.

12   He lies over the grass.
     The stone is cold.
     He makes a deep deep hole
     and plants his pipe.
     The cat is free, the man
     has got a job,
     the house becomes a place
     in which a crow
     flapping from room to room
     whistles her maiden name.

Still Lives

The student in this picture is my father
in the first Cambridge apartment,
bent over his thesis on Cézanne.
I think of a man arranging oranges
at breakfast, trying to understand
how light fell from the dull window
upon lemons, what color the shadows were
that yellow fruit cast on a blue cloth.
His wife was the lady that took dictation
at the Peabody Museum, famous for glass flowers.
Her desk was behind the arctic zone
where a stuffed polar bear forever yawned,
its throat dark as a closet.
Beneath her, where I never went alone,
a giant squid hung suspended, long
tentacles over the basement corridor.
The young Admiral Peary, adrift on an ice floe,
I watched her type out the afternoon
next to an artificial weasel whose coat
turned white in winter, russet again in spring.
I turned a dial and the snow fell for weeks
and weeks. It buried the imperfect world,
it made the white bear and the walrus
move on the pack ice, it made
the ice heave and break up in the sun.

No one in my house has ever died.
My father still arranges lemons
in another light, his father stands behind
as an old merchant, offering wax fruit
with his foxy smile, seeing if I will bite.
Even the undertaker is there, great uncle
on my mother's side, his furrowed face
like a map of rivers, his hands worn smooth
from so many years' handling the dead.
They pull down curtains on the afternoon
as it grows darker. They go to the window
when it begins to snow. My grandmother,
who never speaks, puts down her mystery
and watches as the lights of my own car
enter the driveway. He is coming home,
their prodigal, he has been out
where it is living and he brings
messages from a world.
There are no miracles, he says,
but he knows better. He has seen
things happen they would not believe,
which he will tell them after he digests
a little something, when the time
comes to say where he has been.

Picking Up a Spoon

A long, ritual preparation
before the act: pulling the skin
over the hand like a warm glove,
stalking the spoon itself as if
it were a leopard in green brush,
without concern, as Krishna said,
for the fruits of action,
the end result,
the dish of pineapple
in the mirror, the pears
standing expectantly on end.

The spoon stands in one place
appearing to be dead.
The man paces the floor
smoking cigars,
he watches the sun crawl
across the morning.
Any ape would do better,
King Kong, decisively
seizing his instrument
and eating everything around,
fruit, bowl, hunks
of his own flesh
then falling into
a dreamless primate sleep.

While he was thinking
it began to dance.
Nothing fancy,
kind of a hornpipe,
heel and toe,
all that a spoon could
do without a hand.
He watched in horror.

Finally it all grew clear.
He knew how it was done.
He reached and closed the hand
in one dimension.
The spoon was his,
useful, concave and round.
He called for food,
the boy brought meats
and turnip. Their bodies
grew full and happy
as a pair of owls
under the cold moon.

He held his face
to the spoon,
which showed the truth:
grotesque nose
and shrunken eyes
as treacherous as pigs'
the beard inverted,
pubic and complex.

The walls opened
and closed,
he grew handsome
as Christ, aligned
the nose upon the face
under and between
the eyes, where
it should be.
The spoon
controlled the world.
It was the partner
in his little dance,
shuffling around
his room.

Taken from Van Gogh

He was a hunter before painting crows.
He worked in their own open country,
the cornfield, the three windmills by the sea
slowly revolving in that summer light.
It is impossible to tell the truth
so he presents an ear
wrapped in brown paper like a bun.
Rachel accepts it.

The crows come down. They perch along the wires
by the track. For Rachel, they are as a staff
of notes, a black arpeggio
when his shots scatter them to flight,
an old song when they come back one by one
to rest. Not with a picture of the world
will she begin, but with an ear for music,
holding it close like a gift from a strange man
with a Dutch accent and paint-crusted hands.

After the first few customers, her body
felt unreal. The world is born for us
when an astronomer reveals the sun
itself not to be real. Rachel could keep
the ear in the depths of her hope chest,
or she could feed it to her crow, what would
it matter? Vincent is broke and crazy,
the hospital's tilted, the olive trees
wave arms like dancers. Nights like these
the lost ear hears, the amputee
feels his old feet dance in the weather,
crows gather at the window ledge, each
bearing a message from the sea.

To put it another way, with the tide out
a few crows by the shore make a dark scene:
black rocks, wet sand, a turgid sky
reflected in the sea. You listen
but there is nothing, neither the caws
of spring nor the aggressive croaks
around the summer nest. It is as if
you could not hear, even with your head
cocked toward the good side.
Follow the logic of that silence
to its end, and it will be the sun
blaring and yellow as a marching band.

Or you could think of all the crows as specks
in Rachel's eye, messed up
by tears as she stands there alone
among the girls, sad and embarrassed
by the mute token of his affection.

Art is a puzzle. He turns around
and paints himself on the bad side
with his pipe. He paints the sun,
paints crows, a church, then goes
insane and dies. They make arrangements
for the last group canvas: Rachel with
the ear, the sun, vivid and smiling
on the left, the crows, in mourning
in the near background. You,
the reader, dressed in Vincent's clothes,
sit in the corner and the book you hold
is a long treatise about the self.

Truth is a mirror, where we hear
the crows in yellow and the sun
in black. A new self-portrait: this time
with razor, Rachel beside us,
black birds floating over the wild wheat
that road traveling up and nowhere
the bed tipped toward us like an evil dream.
Trying to reach the heart, trying to give,
we slice off pieces of ourselves like fruit,
we walk into a night where stars
are pictures, falling where they seem.

The Equinox and After

April is here again and dancing beside us
like an old athlete in a bearskin suit.
It forces us into new trajectories,
it opens its fist into a brace of fingers
and we recoil in fear like virgins, having seen
the origins of life and drawing back
to solitary beds. A branch brushes the screen
with sounds like moth wings and with new odors
that might be called harmonies of the night.

Winter was a long novel read by kerosene
beside the stove. It had too many heroes.
The plot was thick and lacked resolution.
The ones we loved married the wrong people,
the ones we despised prospered, the boring ones
held forth for chapters and refused to die.

After a dream season in a quilted bed
it is now April with its warm realities
like a bright morning when you thought
you had been reading the entire night
and wake with one of the characters beside you
in hot natural sleep, the signs around
of a night of love, a whole winter of love.
You think that it might all have been real,
that the dull winter and your whole pointless life
had sizzled with erotic heat, while you
slept through it like a grotesque human bear.

It is Daylight Savings Time and you believe
you are insane again and no one exists,
only yourself and your obscure desires
for chocolates and sleep. You turn
the pages of a book to find them there
with dark eyes and the wet bodies of seals.
You demand to be transposed to another form
so you can welcome April properly
but all too late. It is here already, splendid
with sappy dances and extravagant birds
but not for you. It is the birthday party
of the world and you are the downstairs tenant,
beating your broom against the ceiling
for a calm orderly place in which to read.
For it is all real, even in your wicked bones
you feel the sunlight and you know the crows
have plucked out the old eyes of Death again
and the long corpses begin to rise and dance,
the crowd comes towards you and there is no choice,
your throat begins to sing, your gross physique
moves with that music of its own accord,
the time being here for time to begin again.

Dentist

The good dentist gives me nitrous oxide
and lowers a small fox into my mouth.
I think of a long poem by Chaucer
in a peculiar language, while the fox
chews at the soft root of my tooth,
then lies down for the winter
under my tongue. There is an evil taste,
I spit out some red fox hairs.
Outside the window it is Christmas
in Minneapolis. The fire hydrants
lift up their arms from the snow,
the red and blue mailbox sings
from its hinged mouth a single note
that rises over an entire city
of frozen lakes, over the famous
river where the poet died.
After my tooth is gone, something
begins to fall from the air.
I hold my hands out and they fill
with hundreds of small letters.
I study their curious postmarks
in alphabets that look like Cyrillic
and Greek, their old stamps
with the faces of Sacco and Vanzetti,
of Ulysses S. Grant, Friedrich Engels,
Leon Trotsky and Francis Scott Key.
They are addressed to the man
in the upstairs apartment
who walks heavily after midnight,
who has no teeth in his head at all
and sleeps, like a fox, during the day.

Five Translations from the Poems of Anasim Miscjek

Translator's Note: These are, of course, translations without originals, Miscjek being perhaps the idea of a Rumanian poet.

The Commissars

The commissars are starting to count again.
They are counting how many angels
can stand on the head of a pin.
Their wives live in bourgeois apartments
where they count pins, count them and stack them
by tens and hundreds and thousands
till they fill one of the guest bedrooms,
leaving no space for angels
or anything incorporeal.
In the evening, at home,
one of the commissars asks of his wife
what she keeps in the room with the locked door.

It is an angel, she says, an angel
with diaphanous wings, with the face of her father
who died in the last days of the Uprising.
It is an angel circling the light like a moth,
whose wings are the color of death, an angel
that no longer flies but writes in a grave book
the names of certain citizens of the state.

Next morning he is late to the office.
His work is begun already by a mere
bureaucrat, his usual chair is taken.
He descends into the street as an ordinary man:
the question of angels and pins
will proceed without him.

Angel

Fat bird, unstable angel, it is for you
I walk the streets after curfew at my own peril.
It is for you I throw my cloak over my face,
a map of pain transformed by the full moon.

Under the collective landscape is an old city,
restless and Transylvanian.
Beneath my pleasant and loquacious shape
is a man with hair growing between the eyebrows,
a man with hair over his entire face,
with cloven satanic hooves and teeth like fangs.

It is difficult to suppress a culture.
For every place they try to push it down
it springs up in another. Aristocrats
from the former regime wander the streets.
They are disguised as efficient workers,
as servile obedient poets; but at night
they are lycanthropes. They pass through the crowd
with their sanguinary obsessions.

Beloved, my sacred and profane animal,
I stroll on the hot boulevards because of love.
Of all the disarmed citizenry only I
carry the soft, private weapon of insurrection.
I guard your apartment like the secretest of police.
I will be there when the sun rises over the Danube.
I will be there when fresh patrols relieve
the tired, official guardians of the night.

To His Brother in America

Who knows what trash mother was sleeping with
when she bore you, bastard defector,
torturer of cats in the old neighborhood,
teat-sucker, Doctor of Languages,
exile, escapee, evader, usurper,
my deserter, my likeness? And what
svelte pupils sit on your fat knees
at that pseudouniversity?
It is your brother speaking, the one
with the bestial habits, the Marxist
mill-laborer, the fraternal skeleton
dining again on maggoty potatoes,
illiterate poet
and sleeping with the same old sows.
I walk in Dragovil street with wet shoes,
I apologize for you, I excuse you
as a prisoner invents excuses for his cellmate,
each night covering with blankets a pile of stones
when the guard comes, even for months
after the escape.

Prison Song

Forty years back they kept Jews here;
it was a minor stopover of the Holocaust.
The wall of my cell carries their old inscriptions
in heiratic alphabets that I translate
one to the other till I reach my own
like a scholar using the Rosetta stone:
names, dates where they had come from, where,
when they got out, they were told they were going.
Being half Jew myself, half suburb-of-Bucharest,
I come here regularly on sedition counts
as a banker would spend vacations at the spa.

The man at the entrance takes my watch and cash
as they did in the Old days; but no questions now
as to my race or my religion, no examining
the length of my nose, no getting out the penis
for evidence of a ritual circumcision.
They ask if I believe in the People's state;
I answer that I will when they let me out.

They give a uniform and assign me to the shop
where I bind books. A week of this and I recant.
In such a country everything is fair.
On leaving, it is a cousin on my father's side
that smiles politely, returning my watch
and my gold tooth, my wallet with all its money.
I ask him whether they gave interest this month,
he laughs and writes my name into his book.
The train, with its quaint coal fire and pistons,
takes me in an hour to my home, my woman
with hot soup, my typewriter and its disloyal work.

Miscjek's Success

The award of a state pension surprised me.
I moved to a remote border province
where orderly farms circle the small town
with its obsolete mayor dribbling in his beard.
Beyond, in the great forest, the barbarians live
like animals, feeding by night,
sleeping in trees by day.
In the morning I find footprints on my lawn,
my fig tree plundered, a trail of seeds
vanishing in the shadows. I sit on my porch
as the barbarians emerge.
I see they have hollowed the heads
of animals to wear on their own heads.

I hear them speaking to one another
as they gather ominously into groups.
Unholy languages drift on the night wind,
one of which is my own. My ears stand up,
I smell something like the smell of blood.
I feel my throat forming the alien sounds.
The old tachycardia returns, the eyes
narrow to slits that could see anything.

I rise up to converse with them, but
remembering my stature and my agreements,
I turn and settle among my books.
The fire Marta thoughtfully prepared
burns in the corner, but the shapes
of animals still dance in the flames;
their feral music
troubles this country air.

California

I think of the California poets,
how easy it is for them.
They have vast open spaces,
they drive jeeps and live nowhere,
they drift from cabin to cabin
on mountains with beautiful Spanish names
and there are girls in the cabins
who love poetry and sleep with the poets freely,
for in California there is no guilt nor shame
nor hunger, life is as a dream,
lobsters crawl up on the shore to be caught,
they shoot seabirds and fry them in butter on the beach.

There are no seasons in California.
You make your own, you move from
places where the sun shines all the time
to places where it rains or snows forever.
If you want June or October or some cross-country skiing,
you go to that place in your jeep
and the season is there always.

It is a good climate for poetry, since it is full
of images. You pluck them from the trees like breadfruit
with your feet or knock them down like coconuts.
It is good also for religion, as the Three Winds
bring secret doctrines from the East,
sensual and voluptuous names for the emotions,
creeds that make holy your underground desires,
your daily habits and the parts of your body.

In New England we scratch in the soil with sticks,
find scarce turnips among the rocks,
have no religion at all, fence out our neighbors,
wear clothes, work hard, abstain from sex
and write poems, when we do, on the way to the madhouse.

I spent some time in the Midwest, where they
were neither wholly free nor wholly tragic.
They lived, screwed, married, divorced and died
like regular folk. They grew corn and fed it to
their pigs, then shipped them east and west
for slaughter. It made sense.
When I am finished with this rocky ground,
wet weather and neurotic ocean,
I will become a Baptist in Des Moines,
rise early and drive over to the river
to watch the fall migrations.
I will take photographs and keep
a family album, write no poems, for poems,
Maine or California, drive you crazy.

A Station of Monet

Another season descends
on this cold landscape.
I sit at the table before breakfast
considering Monet, our grand tour
of looking at Monets, twelve countries,
forty senior citizens and us,
the last thing we did together
and enjoyed.
He was intrigued with railroads,
two canvases at least of the great
Gare Saint-Lazare, one in Chicago
and the bright sunlit station in Prague
where the man stopped you
and pressed papers into your hand.

Light enters through translucent flesh
hung on a steel skeleton,
a body in four dimensions
inhabited by spiders.
This is the light in which
time is incessantly becoming space
and long trains arrive
out of the past,
turn on a great wheel
inside the station,
whistle and depart
into the future, carrying
new groups of travelers
to the next museum.

I think I will call you up to say
the others are probably all dead,
it is all altered, that upstairs
a different woman sleeps,
like you, with one ear open,
listening for coffee.

I lose individual paintings,
which ones were in the Marmottan
which were in Belgrade.
We kept them alive for a while
quizzing each other in bed
then that too stopped.
From the possibilities of time,
irrational details:
the screech of exhaling pistons,
the steam rising through ironwork;
at the roofpeak the small falcon,
its wings refracting the sun.
The feeling of steel upon steel,
all the contact of hands
in former cities.

Running in Winter

1   Now, even at the solstice, darkest week,
the fugitive sun trapped under a stone,
I run through the streets of this small town.

My grey, hooded body startles the Christmas
shoppers. They stare. They think it is a man
riding an animal out of the cold future;

in their holiday season they have placed fires
upon the trees, and, in the sky, deliberate
fires transect the field of night. I look up,

running, at a moon with the austere face
of Franz Schubert. It is true. This is
the music, these are the seven concentric spheres.

Inside the houses it has become absolute
zero. The air is liquid. The families flow
slowly from room to room, all of them reading

aloud from "A Child's Christmas in Wales."
The parents falter with age, but the tongues
of children are separate and vivid flames.

2   A man carried a tree through the public street.
He sang, to himself, fragments of a cantata
on the origins of song. He had been handsome,

he had been sexual. He had loved a woman
with two names, in fact, two separate bodies.
That was his tragedy. Now he had something wrong,

a kind of leprosy. He moved as if in pain.
Seeing his need, seeing he was unique,
the people threw coins over the snow and ran.

Only the children watched him, from a grid
of ivory faces, like angels, like a chorus
of the dead. The song went on. A generation

of silence must be borne. These are the last
humans. These are the deep, purifying snows.
That man was not the prophet, but he had

a clear voice opening the night, stopping
the shoppers in their tracks. Say this:
He brought his tree into an empty house,

trimmed it with living birds and lighted
them on fire. It was a night remembered
by the citizens. They had seen a burning house,

they had heard singing and had grown afraid.
In the morning they found bones of a man's
death. Over him lay dozens of charred birds.

3 This is the real winter. The animals return
from the river bottoms and the high fields.
They are drawn crudely, as in primitive

paintings of the Flood and the Creation.
The cows look natural, but the yaks and camels
are something else, as if the artist's hand

made them from travelers' descriptions.
In the last house on the road, after their work,
a woman and man make love by the lighted tree.

It is a voluntary act. Everything else they know
has been obscured. They know each other. They have
named the creatures gathered outside their door,

they have named all the watchers, and they know
what will come to pass, the generations of blood,
the long, waiting centuries. When it is over,

she falls asleep but he keeps talking of the sun,
of the day when they will all be free, windows
and doors removed, the livestock wandering

through the rooms, the rain pouring down and spring
attacking the land with its raw fingers,
its tongue, its grotesque and blossoming heart.

Romance

1. The sunflower is a virgin
with chocolate eyes.
Her green body
is a thin tongue
out of the earth.
She is the death princess
of the garden; her drum
holds images of snakes
on its taut head.
She summons the fog
like a familiar,
she weaves the trees
into each other,
into the heart
of the woman watching
from the garden window.

   She stands among cucumbers.
Her thoughts are earthworms
mulching the warm soil.
When she was young,
lovers resembled each other
like the fall warblers.
Now they are night migrants
speaking the same sweet cry.

2. In the morning she would wish
for wings
so she could follow them
beyond the Caribbean
to Yucatan.
She leans against her hoe,
her bones
no longer hollow.
Behind the eyelids,
white butterflies
circulate in pairs.

A man would go blind
sketching this landscape
he would go mute
knowing the names of these plants,
meeting the sunflower
like a man meeting his bride
for the first time.
He has known her forever
but he is still naked;
while the green habit of summer
covers her full body,
pregnant, by the male
of another species.
They have spoken the nuptials
in a foreign language.
He fails to understand.

3   The romance of the farmer
and his plant
consumes them both.
In love
the scythe slices the grass,
in love the knife
opens the firm fruit.
Vegetarians are known
to be the cruelest husbands.
They enter their lovers
with sharp instruments,
they spill their seed
on the bare ground.

Eating the thing you love
leaves a strange taste
in the mouth.
It inflames the tongue
until you lose the gift
of speech, until you return
to the long silence
of the original person
in the lost garden,
vacant of knowledge,
a simple cell
of the first waters,
beating its heart
in time.

The *Grand Design*

I come to the sea thinking of human loss.
Two centuries ago the *Grand Design*,
crowded with Irish immigrants, struck

on the half-tide ledge where I now stand
in June, a couple of boats in the swell,
white gulls haunting the place in pairs,

in threes and fours: the families
of the dead. It is still their place
to cry the lost names into the wind.

The past invades the present till we can
no longer say *I* or *them*, this century
or that. The first station in the *Book*

of the Dead is a white light, clear
and blinding, like the sun itself
here at the solstice, suspended naked

in pure sky. Everything remains:
The same birds scream, the same species
moves restlessly over the Atlantic,

Ireland to Pennsylvania, Pennsylvania
to Ireland, pelagic migrants, hungry
for new lands, hungry for transformation.

In the northwest corner of the brain,
the yellow goddess Shandhali tearing a head
from a corpse, one hand holding a heart

the other putting a corpse up to her mouth.
We know by now that she is our own self.
The black fox-headed one, her left hand

holding an intestine, a razor in her right;
the greenish black elephant-headed one,
drinking blood from a skull, all of them

they will come chewing on their nether lip,
their eyes will be glassy, their hair tied
over their heads, big-bellied, narrow-waisted,

holding the karmic record book. They will inquire
how we lived; from our answers
they will assign us our next lives.

The knowledge-holding deities will be there,
holding our skulls, the life of the body being gone,
the mind moving alone through its own time.

The *Grand Design* leaned like a whale hulk
for weeks, its spars crusted with salt ice,
then broke in timbers. These are the elements.

Water and rock collide, the sun burns
in the air. It seems we have lived before,
as immigrants in the dark hold of a ship,

immigrants dazzled by the wilderness
or a strange city. It seems that we exchange
bodies for a moment and then labor on

like birds stemming the wind. There is no end
to the design. Death is a blue figure
somewhere in the tapestry, like a mistake

in the deep background, an accident
skillfully rewoven as a ship
with passengers, a fabulous, full-rigged ship
to carry passengers into the New World.

Poem on His Birthday

It is difficult to find presents
for the man who has nothing.
Whatever you bring to his room
he accepts, and it is still empty.
You could bring him a horse
and it would vanish between cracks
into a vacant cellar.
You could bring baskets of light
and it would be dark.
You could bring an expensive watch.
When you got to his driveway
it would begin running backward
faster and faster, till the hands
spiraled away like a pair of swifts.
You could bring nothing
thinking that if he had so much
he would want more.
If you brought nothing,
it would mean coming naked
to a room where a more naked man
sat on the floor, it would mean
seeing the only thing he ever had
how it was exactly like what you had
when you began, when it was everything.

The Hours of Morning

1. You are asleep.
   Craftily, I unhook
   your nightgown.
   A breast appears
   like an owl
   from a dead tree,
   an owl with one round eye
   which I eat, privately,
   then fly to my own house.

2. These are shadows,
   these are birds, these
   are the shadows of birds
   circling in an airshaft.
   I think I have grown a shrike's beak
   and the hooked claws of a shrike.
   It is an hour when
   I have to touch something.
   I reach to you without arms,
   I wake and it is another room
   filled with a sound like wings.

3. We are all at the headwaters
   of the Nile.
   The man dressed as an undertaker
   explains that in his normal life
   he is a priest
   and has no penis.
   The people gather like storks
   along the shore.
   We speak with them;
   they answer in guttural croaks.
   They stir the waters with their feet,
   probing for frogs.

4   For generations
    we have had insomnia.
    I think of the man
    in the last hour;
    he could have been Osiris
    whose member had been devoured
    by a fish.
    To write this in my book of dreams
    I light a candle,
    then move it to your eyes
    which will shift back and forth
    if you are dreaming.
    In that experiment
    I set fire to a strand of hair.

    Retreating, I watch my own face
    in an empty glass.
    It is the face of Thoth,
    patron of writing. It is
    the ibis head of that ludicrous god.

5   This is the darkest hour.
    The moon has set,
    the sun hangs over Afghanistan
    lighting its barbarous noon.
    The thrush has already begun.
    The song of the thrush is a man
    and woman carrying oboes into the trees.
    They stop,
    they play certain ecstatic chords,
    at intervals they hold their instruments
    in rapt attention.
    Others try on their voices
    just before dawn, but the hermit thrush
    is the true prophet. Only his singing
    designs the silence.

6   At sunrise, you conceive
    of what you are.
    You see it breaching the horizon
    and you say, this is the sun,
    that is the self.
    Only at first are you surprised to hear
    those measured footsteps on the roof:
    great black-backed gulls
    walking in contemplation of the dawn
    like monks.
    It is the hour of certainty,
    what was unreal during the night
    vanishes or takes shape.
    Beside you, on her face,
    the dawn traces another landscape.

7   Pirates overwhelm Milwaukee
    Orioles lick Angels
    Royals annihilated by Reds
    Blue Jays fall twice.
    My cat brings, as a gift,
    a severed squirrel's head.
    The ghost of Darwin is a crow,
    the ghosts of Einstein
    and Niels Bohr are crows.
    All crows are ghosts;
    they walk from branch to branch
    like alchemists.
    They hang restlessly
    in the wind.

8   I stand stark naked
    in the long mirror.
    I observe that the body
    is an elephant
    whose sensitive trunk noses the world
    as a blind scholar reads, his fingers
    hovering over the braille,
    the last elephant somewhere in a cave
    decoding petroglyphs.
    Outside, the trees
    hunch toward the wind like bats.
    At what level of perception are we blind,
    asked the philosopher, for in the mirror
    we see everything.

9   At breakfast, life is as a farm
    in autumn, not in the time of copulation
    but in the time of harvest, the fields
    fat with cereals and grain.
    I am a fox now entering the henhouse
    I am a fox eating the sweet eggs
    of birds, I am a fox
    in the gardens of anarchy
    where creatures eat of themselves
    and change, one into the other,
    climbing the food chain,
    climbing the Great Chain of Being
    in which the simplest worms of the damp earth
    come to be angels.
    I am a red fox eating angels.
    It is the hour of predation and the sheep
    gather around the window.
    They have given themselves
    that their predators may be changed,
    that all things may be changed,
    changed utterly
    and in the twinkling of an eye.

10 His friends arrive with their binoculars.
    They startle him, costumed for ornithology
    like that, talking among themselves
    of the Barred Owl and the Red-throated Loon.
    He is in business clothes already, suited up
    for the day's commerce and the cool traffic
    of the Exchange. He has prepared a face
    for market. It is a grave temptation
    and a plot. He falls. He leaves his house
    in the prime sun and in the world
    there are new species everywhere.
    In the Peterson guide the birds sit straight
    like passengers. There is no book
    scanning the real event,
    no taxonomy of change, no language
    for the particularities of life,
    brown birds multiplying in the swamps
    finches evolving from light gray to violet,
    from violet back again to gray.
    He puts his book under a tree.
    He walks, attentive, in the actual day.

11 The city is a hospital without patients.
    Millions of doctors in the streets,
    thousands of doctors taking the subway,
    hundreds of doctors in airplanes
    over the city, piloted by doctors.
    It is no wonder that we are diseased,
    living like this on a remote island,
    living on an island with blue herons
    standing beside the road like guards.
    The island is a hospital without doctors.

Hurrying out of ourselves,
we exchange parts of our bodies,
randomly at first, then forming a square,
then circles within a square, moving,
like a dance, in time.
The herons are also moving
in another pattern, inscrutably
at the edge of things, closer to the sea.

12 In the hot transformations of noon
the sun becomes a bird with a gold eye.
Deep in the shadows a woman of the hour
begins her lunch. It is a world of words
through which I walk in silence
looking at the display, admiring it
as I admire the woman, as I come closer,
finding it to be you, and closer still
finding you are myself, my slender mirror,
a set of wings so tentatively attached
it might be a child's drawing about an angel.
A little conversation and the last hour
is full; I can enter the afternoon
surely, knowing it will be there.

ABOUT THE AUTHOR

William Carpenter was born in Massachusetts and grew up in Waterville, Maine, where he developed an interest in natural history and spent two summers at the Kent Island Ornithological Research Station near Grand Manan, Canada, banding and studying pelagic birds. He graduated from Dartmouth College and took a Ph.D. in English at the University of Minnesota. From 1967 to 1972 he was assistant professor of English and humanities at the University of Chicago. He then returned to Maine to help establish the College of the Atlantic, an experimental institution on an island off the coast of Maine, where he teaches in the Human Studies program.

Deeply interested in the work of Carl Jung, he has taught courses in myth, literature, and the unconscious for the past five years. His poems won the Henry Dumas prize from the *Hiram Review* in 1978. Subsequently they have appeared in the *Beloit Poetry Journal*, the *Black Warrior Review*, the *New England Review*, *Poetry*, *Quarry West*, and *Nimrod*, where "The Yacht" received the Pablo Neruda award in 1979.